The *Shakespeare Library*

A Midsummer Night's Dream

WENDY GREENHILL
HEAD OF EDUCATION,
ROYAL SHAKESPEARE COMPANY

Heinemann Library
Chicago, Illinois

Designed by Green Door Design
Printed in Hong Kong

04 03 02 01 00
10 9 8 7 6 5 4 3 2 1

Library of Congress Cataloging-in-Publication Data
Greenhill, Wendy, 1949-
    A midsummer night's dream / Wendy Greenhill.
      p. cm. -- (The Shakespeare library)
    Includes bibliographical references and index,
    Summary: Introduces Shakespeare's play A Midsummer Night's Dream,
discussing plot and characters, possible sources of inspiration for the play, the history of
early performances, and how the productions have evolved over the years.
    ISBN 1-57572-284-4 (lib. bdg.)
    1. Shakespeare, William, 1564-1616. Midsummer night's dream—Juvenile
literature. 2. Comedy—Juvenile literature. [1. Shakespeare, William, 1564-1616.
Midsummer night's dream. 2. English literature—History and criticism.] I. Title.
PR2827.G74 2000
822.3'3—dc21
                                                          99-054316

Acknowledgments
The authors and publishers would like to thank the following for permission
to reproduce photographs and other illustrative material:

Bridgeman Art Library, p. 6; The British Library, p. 4; Cambridge University Library, p. 7;
Photostage/Donald Cooper, pp. 9, 15, 16; E.T. Archive, pp. 5, 26; RSC Collection, pp 19, 23, 30;
Shakespeare Centre Library/Joe Cocks Studio Collection, pp 8, 10, 11, 13, 17, 20, 21, 25,
27, 29, 31; Tate Gallery, p12; Victoria and Albert Museum, pp 14, 18, 22.

Every effort has been made to contact copyright holders of any material reproduced in this book. Any omissions will be rectified in subsequent printings if notice is given to the publisher.

Names in SMALL CAPS in the text are characters in the play.

Some words are shown in bold, **like this.**
You can find out what they mean by looking in the glossary.

CONTENTS

THE SOURCES

William Shakespeare was a professional actor, a businessman, and a playwright. Today, nearly 400 years after his death, his plays are still performed, moving audiences to tears and to laughter. Shakespeare's works tell us much about **Elizabethan** England. What is most remarkable is that Shakespeare's plays can still tell us something about ourselves.

Shakespeare was attracted by the brightest and best moments in other stories. He explored the most dramatic events in English history, rewrote love stories, and developed known characters. He was able to blend these elements from different sources into new plays. He usually made the stories more exciting and interesting than their originals. Shakespeare wrote in a lively, expressive way that made the audience feel the atmosphere of the places and events on stage and share the feelings of the characters. He and his friends ran one of the most popular theater companies in London. The performances of his and other writer's plays packed in audiences of up to 3,000 people nearly every day

It is encouraging to learn that Shakespeare's plays did not come to him out of nowhere in a flash of inspiration. In the early 1590s, he began writing plays based on English history. A best-selling history book of the time, *Chronicles of England, Scotland and Ireland,* provided most of the information about the kings and other people involved.

The love story of *Pyramus and Thisbe,* portrayed in this 1538 engraving, was told by the Roman poet Ovid. The story appears again in *A Midsummer Night's Dream.*

A few years later, Shakespeare began working with existing romantic and comic stories. There was one book in particular that he knew well from his schooldays. It was called *Metamorphoses* by the Latin poet Ovid. Ovid's stories were about transformations, or changes, that his characters found themselves going through. Sometimes these were frightening, for example, when humans changed into animals. Ovid's stories must have sunk deep into Shakespeare's imagination, because his plays contain many echoes from them.

The story of *Pyramus and Thisbe,* which is used in *A Midsummer Night's Dream,* appears in Book 4 of *Metamorphoses.* It is striking how many details Shakespeare borrowed. He even borrows the crack in the wall through which the two lovers whisper. Pyramus blames the wall.

Jealous wall, why do you stand in the way of lovers?

It is only a little step to make the Wall a character, as Shakespeare does in his play-within-a-play in *A Midsummer Night's Dream.* It is a step that makes Shakespeare's version of the story much funnier.

The strangest transformation in *A Midsummer Night's*

Dream is when BOTTOM is magically given a donkey's head and meets the Queen of the Fairies, who takes a fancy to the transformed Bottom. Shakespeare based this part of his story on another Latin book well-known to the Elizabethans, *The Golden Ass* by Apuleius. *Ass* is another word for donkey. He also used details from several earlier poems that refer to OBERON and TITANIA, King and Queen of the Fairies. Robin Goodfellow, or PUCK as he is usually called in the play, was a mischievous spirit from folklore.

Shakespeare's magic was in how he chose, mixed, and developed elements from these different sources.

The sprite in this seventeenth-century illustration is Robin Goodfellow. He is also known as Puck.

EARLY PERFORMANCES

A PRIVATE FIRST PERFORMANCE?

There is a mystery about the first performance of *A Midsummer Night's Dream*. It seems that the play was written between 1593 and 1596, but it is not known for certain where it was first staged. Many scholars think that it was written for an aristocratic wedding and first performed as part of the celebrations. It is even possible that Queen Elizabeth was guest of honor.

The first copy was printed in 1600.

Several flattering references to her majesty are hidden in the play.

If this theory is true, then on this occasion, Shakespeare was writing for a small, educated audience. The grand house where the wedding party took place would have been richly decorated. We know that the **Elizabethans** loved feasts and dancing, pageants, and spectacular shows of all kinds. The actors would have made the most of the occasion, creating effects that were not possible in the public theaters where they usually worked. They could have used candlelight, for example, and more delicate and complex music.

A PUBLIC SUCCESS

The script of *A Midsummer Night's Dream* was printed in London in 1600. The title page says that the play had been "publicly" acted "sundry times," in other words, quite often. This suggests that even if it had been originally written for a wedding party, *A Midsummer Night's Dream* was later staged in the public theaters to a large, mixed audience and that it was popular. The actors must have thrown themselves into the varied moods of the play and made it a hit.

Enough is known about the design of Elizabethan playhouses to imagine how some of the more tricky moments of action were achieved. There were two

A

Midsommer nights dreame.

As it hath beene sundry times pub-
lickely acted, by the *Right honoura-
ble,* the Lord Chamberlaine his
feruants.

Written by William Shakespeare.

¶ Imprinted at London, for *Thomas Fifher,* and are to
be foulde at his fhoppe, at the Signe of the White Hart,
in *Fleeteftreete.* 1600.

entrances to the stage through doors in the back wall, and they led into dressing room space. The doors provided an exit, a quick change, and an entrance through the other door. This was a perfect way of surprising the audience, for example, when BOTTOM suddenly appears with the donkey head. There was also an alcove covered by a curtain in the back wall. This made a natural place for the Queen of the Fairies' **bower**.

Music and dancing are an important element throughout this play. In Elizabethan times, a band would have played live from the **gallery** above the stage along the back wall.

There are four women's parts in the play and, as usual, boys or young men played those parts. There were no actresses on the Elizabethan stage, but boys were a great success in the female roles. The two girls in the play,

HERMIA and HELENA, are young and lively. They have some marvellous comic moments, including a fight. Imagine a couple of boys, perhaps about twelve years of age, whose voices have not yet changed. They must have had a lot of fun bringing these parts to life.

TITANIA would have been a harder challenge for a young male actor. She speaks some of the most highly descriptive language in the play, and she goes through a range of very strong emotions. She has to be convincing as a fairy of the supernatural world, yet she must also be human in her feelings.

The Elizabethans loved shows and celebrations. This is a water show organized in 1591 to entertain Queen Elizabeth.

THE CHARACTERS

The characters fall into three groups. There are those associated with Duke Theseus and his court; there are the workmen of Athens; and there are the fairies in the wood. The story of the play brings people from each of these groups into contact with each other with comic, romantic, and disturbing results.

THESEUS Duke of Athens, a man of authority. He has just returned triumphant from war against the Amazons.

HIPPOLYTA Queen of the Amazons, a tribe of warlike women. She was defeated in battle by Theseus and brought back to Athens. He intends to marry her. But Hippolyta doesn't agree with the idea, because he was recently her enemy.

This miniature, painted by Nicholas Hilliard in 1590, shows a young nobleman dressed very richly, perhaps for Court or a wedding. The actors playing Lysander and Demetrius would have been dressed like this.

LYSANDER A young nobleman in love with Hermia.

DEMETRIUS Another young nobleman in love with Hermia. He used to love Helena.

HERMIA A rather short young lady who loves Lysander. She has a strict father.

HELENA A tall young lady who loves Demetrius. She is Hermia's best friend. They went to school together.

EGEUS Hermia's father. He wants her to marry Demetrius even though she loves Lysander. He has a temper and is even prepared to see her in a **nunnery** or killed if she disobeys him.

PHILOSTRATE Man in charge of entertainment at Theseus's Court. He has his own ideas about who is suitable to be presented at Court. He is a bit of a snob.

OBERON King of the Fairies. He is a master of magic power and uses it to get his own way.

TITANIA Queen of the Fairies. She is a creature of the wood and in close harmony with the natural world. She and Oberon have had an argument and are avoiding each other at the beginning of the play.

PUCK or ROBIN GOODFELLOW Oberon's chief attendant. He is well-known for practical jokes and general mischief.

PEASEBLOSSOM, COBWEB, MOTH, MUSTARDSEED Fairies in Titania's service.

PETER QUINCE A carpenter and the organizer of the rehearsals for *Pyramus and Thisbe*. He is the man with the difficult task of getting a decent performance out of his actors. He gives out the parts and directs the rehearsals. When they eventually perform at Court, he gives a Prologue that introduces their play to the Duke.

NICK BOTTOM A weaver who plays PYRAMUS. He is the star actor, and he knows it! He is magically changed by Puck, who gives him a donkey's head. He then finds that the Queen of the Fairies has taken a liking to him.

FRANCIS FLUTE A **bellows mender**. He is still quite young, in fact, almost a boy. He boasts that he has a beard beginning to grow and couldn't possibly play a woman's part. Peter Quince insists that Francis Flute play THISBE, the heroine of the story.

TOM SNOUT A **tinker** who plays WALL in the play.

SNUG A **joiner** who plays LION. He says that he is slow at learning lines and is relieved that he only has to roar.

ROBIN STARVELING A tailor who plays MOONSHINE in the play.

WHAT HAPPENS

THESEUS, Duke of Athens, has just returned from fighting against the warlike Amazons. He has brought back their Queen, HIPPOLYTA, whom he wishes to marry.

EGEUS is determined that his daughter HERMIA will marry the young man of his choice, DEMETRIUS. Hermia is in love with LYSANDER. Egeus brings all three young people to see the Duke and begs for his support in forcing them to accept his wishes. Lysander argues that he is just as suitable a husband as Demetrius, with the advantage of being loved by Hermia. What's more, he reminds everyone that Demetrius used to be in love with HELENA, who is now broken-hearted because he has switched his attention to Hermia.

Egeus appeals to an ancient law of Athens that says that a father can arrange his daughter's marriage entirely as he wishes. Theseus agrees that the law does allow this and points out to Hermia the choices she has. She can agree to marry Demetrius as her father wants, she can enter a convent as a nun, or she can die. He gives her a few days to make up her mind.

Lysander and Hermia try to console one another, and Lysander explains his plan. They will run away in the middle of the night and set off for his aunt's house some distance from Athens. He expects to find a welcome there and the chance to marry. And he hasn't forgotten that his aunt is rich!

Helena, Hermia's best friend, appears. Lysander and Hermia tell her what they have decided to do.

Left alone, Helena pours out her feelings. She is miserable because Demetrius ignores her now. She is envious of the love between Hermia and Lysander. She decides to tell Demetrius what they are going to do. She thinks that he will follow them so as not to lose Hermia, and she will follow him. Perhaps he might even be grateful to her.

QUINCE, BOTTOM, AND COMPANY

A group of workmen gathered together by PETER QUINCE are going to rehearse a play to present to the Duke. It will be part of the Duke's wedding celebrations. The play will be the tragic love story of PYRAMUS and THISBE. Quince has some trouble keeping NICK BOTTOM in order. Bottom wants to play all the best parts.

FAIRYLAND

OBERON and TITANIA, King and Queen of the Fairies, are not getting along. Whenever they meet, a furious argument starts. They accuse each other of being unfaithful—in fact, of Oberon loving Hippolyta and of Titania loving Theseus. They quarrel over a little Indian boy, who is one of Titania's followers, and whom Oberon wants as his **page.** Titania won't give him up because she was fond of his mother, who died in childbirth. She points out to Oberon that their quarrel is disturbing the natural cycle of the seasons and that this causes suffering to human life. The harvests are failing, and the weather is topsy-turvy. Oberon doesn't care.

"Ill-met by moonlight, proud Titania." Paul Scofield plays Oberon and Susan Fleetwood plays Titania in the 1982 production for England's National Theatre.

Oberon plots with Puck, his chief fairy attendant, to take revenge on Titania. Puck is to find a flower whose juice has magical properties. Oberon will use it to make Titania fall madly in love with the next living thing she sees. He hopes it will be something vile.

Confusion in the Wood

Hermia and Lysander are tired and have lost their way in the wood. They lie down to sleep.

Demetrius has followed them, but he is angry that Helena has followed him. He threatens violence if she doesn't go away. She is thoroughly miserable.

Puck has brought the love juice to Oberon. He squeezes some of it into Titania's eyes as she sleeps. Oberon has overheard Demetrius and Helena. He pities Helena and wants to make Demetrius love her, so he tells Puck to use the love juice on Demetrius. Puck will recognize Demetrius by his Athenian style of clothing. Puck squeezes the juice onto the eyes of the first Athenian man he finds, but it is Lysander, the wrong man. Lysander wakes, sees Helena, and immediately declares undying love. Helena is annoyed with him, because she thinks he is teasing her.

Hermia wakes after a frightening dream. She is worried to find that Lysander is nowhere in sight.

Rehearsal in the Wood

Peter Quince has called together his company of actors to rehearse in the wood at night away from prying eyes. All of the men, except Bottom, are anxious about the parts they have to learn and the thought of appearing in front of the Duke. But Quince manages to get a rehearsal going. Puck, as an invisible onlooker, decides to have some fun. When Bottom exits behind a tree, Puck transforms him by giving him a donkey's head. Bottom's appearance terrifies his friends, and they run away.

Ill-Matched Couples

To keep up his spirits, Bottom starts singing and wakes up Titania. Since Bottom is the first living thing she sees, she immediately falls in love with him. Her fairies attend to him, and he is escorted off to her **bower**. Puck reports this success to Oberon, who is delighted.

They see Demetrius followed by Hermia. She believes that he must have killed Lysander out of jealousy. Demetrius is still declaring love to Hermia, so Oberon realizes that Puck has made a mistake. He is sent off to find Helena, and Oberon uses the love juice on Demetrius's eyes while he is asleep.

Puck brings in Helena with Lysander in pursuit. Helena is now at wits' end. The noise they make wakes Demetrius, who sees Helena, and, of course, expresses his passionate love for her, too. This is too much for Helena. She does not deserve to be mocked so cruelly.

Bottom and Flute rehearse *Pyramus and Thisbe* in
the 1994 Royal Shakespeare
Company production.

Things are in chaos when HERMIA arrives on the scene. At first Hermia also believes that LYSANDER is teasing her friend, and she asks him to not be so unkind. Lysander answers her so roughly that she realizes that he means it. He now loves HELENA and not her. Hermia turns a furious anger against Helena, whom she accuses of bewitching Lysander and stealing him away from her. This results in one of the most famous and comic fights in English theater. OBERON and PUCK have had a good laugh at the humans' expense.

CONFUSION UNTANGLED

Oberon takes pity on TITANIA's infatuation with BOTTOM and lifts the magic from her. She is glad to leave the strange sleeping creature, a human with an animal head. She and Oberon make up their quarrel. Oberon took the little Indian boy while Titania was occupied with Bottom. Puck lifts the donkey's head off Bottom.

The four lovers have been arranged into two pairs at last and then put to sleep by Puck. They are awakened by the sound of THESEUS's hunting horns to find themselves in early daylight, on the edge of the wood, surrounded by people they recognize. Life seems almost back to normal, and they doubt their strange memories of the past night. They think they must have been dreaming. Theseus rules that they will be married at the same time as he and HIPPOLYTA. Lysander will marry Hermia, and DEMETRIUS will marry Helena. Bottom wakes up alone in the wood. He thinks he has been dreaming.

Back in Athens, PETER QUINCE and the others are gloomy. Bottom has been bewitched and has disappeared. They will be unable to perform their play. When Bottom suddenly appears, they are overjoyed. The show can go on.

CELEBRATIONS AT COURT

The play of *Pyramus and Thisbe* is chosen by Theseus as the entertainment to be presented at **Court** after the wedding. The actors, including poor Peter Quince, are terrified. But Bottom has a wonderful time overacting. The play is supposed to be a tragic love story, but it becomes a **farce**.

There are some critical comments during the performance, especially from the young lovers who are in high spirits. But at the end, the Duke seems to have enjoyed it and he thanks the actors. Bottom leads the company in a lively dance, the **Bergamask**. Bottom, Peter Quince, and the others have fulfilled their ambition. They have performed for the Duke and his Court.

MIDNIGHT

The newly married couples go to bed. As midnight strikes, the fairies arrive in the palace. They bless the house and weave a spell to bring happiness to the marriages.

Puck has the last word in the form of an **Epilogue**. He tells the audience that they have seen nothing more real than a dream. He begs their forgiveness if anything has caused offense, and he asks for their "hands," that is, their applause, to show their appreciation for the performance they have just seen.

"Gentiles, perchance you wonder at this show." Bottom and his friends perform the play of *Pyramus and Thisbe* for the Duke and his Court. Here are Thisbe and Pyramus whispering through the chink in Wall.

THEMES IN THE DREAM

A Midsummer Night's Dream is a wonderful, complicated story full of comedy and surprises for the audience. Shakespeare created characters that are recognized as true to life in all their complexities and confusion. The play is also much more. It creates a world that mirrors our inner world of dreams, longings, and fears. Sometime it is frightening and dangerous. Sometimes it is beautiful. It is a world in which magic happens and prompts the audience to question what magic really is. Is magic the power of our imagination and of our inner desires? This is one of the questions running throughout the play.

The questions that a play presents and the ideas that it develops are often called its themes. The themes of *A Midsummer Night's Dream* could be summed up as mischief, magic, and marriage. These themes are intertwined.

When directors, designers, and actors rehearse a play, they often explore its themes from many different points of view. Eventually decisions are made about how their understanding of the

TITANIA is asleep with BOTTOM, while PUCK and OBERON perform their magical mischief in a 1991 open-air performance in London.

themes of the play will be expressed in the set design, the use of light and color, the style of music and in the performances themselves.

The themes of a play, such as Shakespeare's *Julius Caesar*, are fairly clear. They are about political ideas and the private emotions of friendship, loyalty, and love. *A Midsummer Night's Dream* is a different type of play. Its themes strike the audience in a richly imaginative way. It is a play that tells a story and gives a new experience. Our own inner dream world is touched.

MISCHIEF AND MAGIC

One of the most striking characters in the play is Puck, who is out for all the fun he can get. He enjoys creating chaos, particularly among humans. Puck says,

Lord, what fools these mortals be!

The mischief-making is not simply fun. Oberon, a complex character, shows the common human feelings of jealousy and spite. Titania will not give Oberon the boy he wants, and a fairyland version of tug-of-love begins. Oberon is determined to get what he wants and to punish Titania. He enjoys using his magic to make her fall in love with the "next vile thing" she sees. In fact, this is BOTTOM with the donkey's head.

This turn of events is both comic and grotesque. It is perhaps even cruel. What goes on when Bottom and Titania meet is extraordinary. Bottom is surrounded by flowers and music. He is treated like a king with tiny servants to bring him whatever he desires. He is entertained by a princess

or a spirit. Everything is strange, beautiful, and aimed at pleasure. Yet the magic has a disturbing edge for the audience. Even though Bottom has become an absurd thing, he is part man and part animal, he is being seduced. Titania has fallen in love with him.

When Oberon restores Titania to her normal state, he has gotten what he wanted. He has the little Indian boy. But Titania has been tricked and so has Bottom. Bottom is left with nothing but a memory. Oberon's power is impressive, but it is also dangerous.

MAGIC AND THE WOOD

The fairy world with its magic is connected with the natural world and nighttime. Titania, in particular, is a creature of the woods. She has a **bower**, which is a hidden place beneath the trees. Her fairies are named after plants and other natural things. The fairies have realistic ideas about the dangers of the natural world, such as snakes, but they charm away these dangers. The charm that Titania's fairies cast over the wood is associated with beauty and pleasure. They sing a lullaby to rock Titania to sleep and to ward off danger. The female fairies are close to nature, and they work in harmony with it.

Fairies working in harmony with nature is a very attractive idea, but, as usual with this play, what seems secure becomes disturbing. TITANIA's fairies fail to keep her out of danger. Their lullaby is useless against her main enemy, OBERON. He takes advantage of her sleep to drop the love juice on her eyes.

The difference between Oberon and Titania is made clear when she expresses her concern that their quarrel has disturbed the balance of the seasons. She wants them to create harmony not disruption.

The fairy kingdom is closely connected to the natural world of the woods. Out of this mix comes a kind of magic that causes a state of confusion. The confusion can be comic, tender, disturbing, or beautiful. It is something to be both desired and feared.

MARRIAGE

At the end of the play, three couples marry, and the King and Queen of the Fairies are reunited. At first sight, this might seem like a simple happy ending with true love leading to marriage. But a closer look at the play raises several questions about these relationships. Love and marriage are not, after all, easy to achieve.

THESEUS and HIPPOLYTA are the human equivalents of the King and Queen of the Fairies. But, in contrast, they have no freedom to follow their own desires.

At the opening of the play, we see them waiting for their wedding. Theseus is impatient for the day to come, Hippolyta says very little and appears to be reluctant. They seem closer during the scene in the woods in the early morning when they are both enjoying the hunt. During the final scenes at **Court,** their conversation flows more freely, but there is never any sense of real love between them.

For the four young people,

The course of true love never did run smooth.

At first their story is about the pains of infatuation. At the end, it seems they may have learned more about themselves and that perhaps now they are ready for love. But this is not certain.

When the fairies come at midnight to bless the house and the marriages, they spread "glimmering light" and "field dew" gifts from their world of magic and nature. These enrich the marriages that have just begun.

Wealthy **Elizabethans** enjoyed arranging private entertainment in their houses for their guests. This is a section from a painting of 1596 that celebrates the life of Sir Henry Unton. It shows the interior of his house with a **masque** (musical entertainment) taking place. It is an occasion like the one that Philostrate arranges for Theseus, Hippolyta, and their guests after their wedding.

DIRECTORS' PERSPECTIVES

THE ROLES OF THE DIRECTOR AND DESIGNER

A Midsummer Night's Dream has been frequently performed. It fascinates directors and designers and is a favorite with audiences.

The director of a production guides the development of all the actors' performances through the rehearsal process. The director has overall responsibility for the interpretation of the play. This involves a detailed look at the **text** of the play. In *A Midsummer Night's Dream*, one fundamental decision to be made is how to portray the FAIRIES and the woods. There are also choices to be explored with the actors about their characters. For example, how cruel is OBERON in his treatment of TITANIA? Is BOTTOM mainly a figure of fun or someone more complex and sympathetic?

In making these decisions, the director has to work closely with the designer who creates the visual aspects of the production. This designer will make basic decisions about the shape and layout of the stage, the points of exit and entrance, and possible platforms and different levels for the actors to use.

One of the challenges for any designer of this play is to create flexible acting space that is suitable for the three groups.

- THESEUS's **Court**
- the rehearsals of PETER QUINCE and his friends
- the world of the fairies and the woods

MAX REINHARDT

Max Reinhardt was a German director who directed 22 of Shakespeare's plays. He directed *A Midsummer Night's Dream* in twelve separate productions. The first was in Berlin, Germany, in 1905. The final one was his famous Hollywood movie of 1935. Reinhardt was fascinated by the play. He constantly found new ideas to explore.

His earliest production created an on-stage forest of real tree trunks and branches and a carpet of moss. A later production in 1910, at the large Deutsches Theater in Berlin continued with magnificently real woods, but also used the latest technical theater devices. The Deutsches Theater had a huge revolving stage. This structure was like a giant turntable. Different scenes could be set up on it in advance. A great advantage of the revolving stage for *A Midsummer Night's Dream* was the speed with which the scene could be changed. While the audience saw Theseus in his Court at the beginning of the play, the woods was ready to be put in place with a turn of the stage.

Reinhardt also used a cyclorama and an electric wind machine to create spectacular on-stage effects. A cyclorama is a curving back wall or curtain. It is usually white. Special lighting effects can be created on the wall. Thousands of light bulbs were fitted behind the cyclorama to create a starry sky. Reinhardt used the new theater technology to create his own form of magic.

PUCK leads the lovers through a forest of real trees in Max Reinhardt's 1905 production.

BEYOND REALISM

In London in 1900, there was a production by Henry Beerbohm Tree that featured real rabbits nibbling real grass. It was a great success, but soon directors and designers developed other ideas.

The influential director and Shakespearean scholar, Harley Granville Barker, believed that the text of the play was the most important. He didn't want the audience looking at the set rather than listening to the actors. So the designs he used were less detailed and did not attempt to look like real places.

He worked with the designer Norman Wilkinson. Together they gave a completely new look to the FAIRIES. **Victorian** productions usually had pretty stage pictures with fairies dressed in droopy white dresses. Wilkinson covered them in gold make-up and dressed them in costumes that looked East Indian. The costumes included jeweled turbans and colorful scarlet and mauve skirts.

Barker was most original in the way he created the forest. A curtain of very fine fabric was drawn across the stage so that it hung in loose folds. It was painted in shades of gold with a dappled, abstract pattern that suggested trees and leaves. He also experimented with the lighting and flooded the stage with bright white light from lamps attached to the front of the **dress circle** of the theater.

The fairies dance their final dance in Harley Granville Barker's production in 1914.

MODERN PRODUCTIONS

Sir Peter Hall directed *A Midsummer Night's Dream* three times on stage and once on film. He was also the first director of Benjamin Britten's opera version of the play. Peter Hall and his designers always located the play within the set of an **Elizabethan** country house and its surroundings. Their aim has been

to take The Dream *back to its beginnings, perhaps for a wedding in a country house.*

Shakespeare set his story in ancient Athens, yet all the descriptions of the woods are like the Warwickshire, England, countryside where he grew up. BOTTOM, QUINCE, and the others are the types of men Shakespeare would have known in Stratford, where his father was a glove maker. Peter Hall's productions have always emphasized the Englishness of the atmosphere.

The transformation of the stage setting from THESEUS's house to the woods has been achieved in various ingenious ways. In the set of Peter Hall's 1959 production, the floor of an Elizabethan manor house was covered with rushes, and there was an upper minstrels' gallery. Gauze, painted with the front view of the house, hung at **gallery** level. Gauze is a very fine sheet of netting, which, when painted, looks solid when it is lit from the front, but disappears from view completely when lit from behind. Changing the direction of lighting on the gauze had the effect of making it disappear. So, in a second, the audience saw not the house but trees and bushes in a soft, misty light receding to the back of the stage. The two worlds of THESEUS's **court** and the fairies' woods were both present.

Peter Hall's production in 1959 was played on the set of an Elizabethan manor house.

ACTORS' PERSPECTIVES

PLAYING THE COMEDY

Directors in this century have enjoyed creating new settings and meanings for *A Midsummer Night's Dream*. Actors have a different challenge. They must bring to life words that were written 400 years ago. They must recreate the comic situations and make them funny for a twentieth-century audience.

Cheek By Jowl Theater Company created a very strong situation for the comic characters in its modern-dress production in 1985. It presented PETER QUINCE, BOTTOM, and the others as typical members of an amateur dramatic society. It was a parody that used common types of personalities. The audience laughed in recognition of the types of people they saw on stage.

There was the terribly serious actor who withdrew into a corner to meditate before rehearsal, and an overly enthusiastic Bottom in a clerical collar. This was the Reverend Nick Bottom, the local vicar who thought of himself as an actor. The actor Colin Wakefield succeeded in making Bottom both very funny and likeable.

In Peter Brook's production, done in Stratford in 1970, the workmen-actors were played not as instantly recognizable types from everyday life. Instead they were portrayed as fully rounded people. The comedy they achieved was gentle. The audience did not laugh at them, but rather at the anxieties and little weaknesses that they shared with the characters.

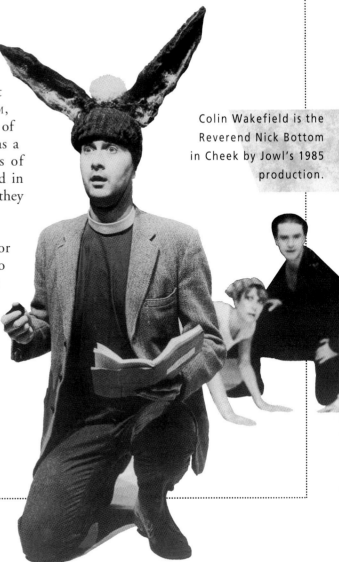

Colin Wakefield is the Reverend Nick Bottom in Cheek by Jowl's 1985 production.

IMPROVISATION AND THE UNEXPECTED

The actor David Waller, who played Bottom in Peter Brook's production, has talked about the use of improvisation and games in rehearsal. He used these techniques to explore what it would be like to be transformed, as Bottom is, into a donkey. He also explored what it would be like to see your friend so shockingly changed. Improvisation is an exercise used to dig deep into a situation or feeling in a play. The actors don't use the words in the play, but freely create the scene with their own words and actions. David Waller wrote,

We did an enormous number of quite extraordinary improvisations on the theme of transformed nightmares in magic woods . . .
trying to think what would actually happen . . .

The result was that the audience shared the other actors' shock. They watched, fascinated, as Bottom, costumed in a black nose and large donkey's ears sticking through his cap, gradually acted more and more as an animal. He pawed the ground with his foot. All his movements changed and finally, he let out a terrifying and convincing ee-oohh, the bray of a donkey. He continued to let out this sound at moments throughout his speech, which was both comic and unnerving.

In 1989 the director John Caird achieved a box office success with his exuberant production. The FAIRIES wore tattered ballet tutus with boot-like shoes. At odd moments they would settle down to read comic books. The actor Richard McCabe played PUCK as a cult hero who signed autographs for his fairy fans. Rather than singing TITANIA to sleep, the fairies had a disco. The comedy in these performances was achieved by wit and the unexpected.

The **bower** of Titania (Claire Higgins) was an old brass bed, and her fairies read comic books in John Caird's 1989 production.

PLAYING THE FAIRIES

In the nineteenth century, the parts of PUCK and OBERON were usually played by young actresses. Ellen Terry, who went on to be the greatest Shakespearean actress of her generation, played Puck at the age of eight. Her first entrance was through a trap door while seated on a mushroom. Other female Pucks and Oberons were elegant to look at, but had little personality.

Actors in the twentieth century have reclaimed the parts of Oberon and Puck. They usually play them as strong, complex, male characters.

The choices to be made about how to play Puck are part of the exploration of the whole fairy kingdom. Peter Hall's three productions presented the fairies as more earthy and natural than the humans. Hall's Puck was closest of all to the animal world. When Ian Holm played the role, he panted eagerly like a dog and sniffed the air for human scent. He was an interesting contrast to Oberon, played by Ian Richardson with great elegance of voice and movement. Puck was of the earth, but this Oberon was aristocratic, the obvious master of the fairy kingdom and all its powers.

TITANIA and her fairies had a different quality. They could charm and weave spells. Titania, played by Judi Dench, had a natural beauty. In a film version of the production, she played the role of Titania almost naked. She was very much a creature of the wood. Judi Dench also gave the character of Titania a sense of humor and fun. For example, Dench's Titania was delighted and almost laughing at herself as she realized how much she had fallen in love with the donkey-headed Bottom.

Ellen Terry played Puck.

Peter Brook's famous 1970 production, set on an all-white stage, presented the fairies as a tight group. There were only four fairies, and they were physically quite large. They were the unseen spirits who caused mischief and confusion at every opportunity. They made the woods an unsettling place for the four lovers, in which there were strange noises and things that mysteriously moved and disappeared. The fairies were a menacing reminder of the uncertainty of life.

Theseus/Oberon, Hippolyta/Titania

Several recent productions have had one actor playing both Theseus and Oberon and one actress playing Hippolyta and Titania. This is called doubling. Peter Brook explained,

The couples are so closely related that we felt that Oberon and Titania could easily be sitting inside the minds of Theseus and Hippolyta.

The fairies in the wood have more freedom, more fun, and more pleasure than people do in ordinary life. Oberon and Titania are like each other. They are the freer sides of Theseus and Hippolyta, the sides which are expressed in fantasies and dreams.

John Carlisle played Theseus/Oberon in 1989. He wore large pointed ears and little fairy wings as Oberon and combined flowing, dramatic speaking of the verse with a tremendous sense of fun. His Theseus, in contrast, was formal and restrained.

In Peter Hall's 1969 movie, the fairies were "earthy,. . . their flesh green-grey like moss and soil."

A FAIRY STORY
FOR ADULTS

The theatrical history of *A Midsummer Night's Dream* reflects the changing tastes and interests of audiences. Each new generation of actors has recreated the play for its own time. This great range of interpretations shows the play's richness.

"Lord what fools these mortals be!" OBERON, PUCK, and TITANIA, three tough characters, bewildered the humans in Peter Brook's production.

Many children are taken to see *A Midsummer Night's Dream* as their first Shakespeare play. Its comedy and the story of the fairies and the young lovers are entertaining for even quite young children.

It is a mistake, however, to think of *A Midsummer Night's Dream* as just charming and simple. As with traditional fairy stories, there are elements in the play that can disturb us. We can enjoy the pretend aspect of the theater on one level and be disturbed by a strange or twisted view of reality on another. A successful production of the play will both entertain and unsettle the audience. It will make us think.

OBERON's pleasure in tricking TITANIA with the love juice is sometimes shown as violent and sexual. All the women in the play suffer to some extent from dominating, cruel men. The confusion of the lovers is also more than simply comic, their whole perception of life and their own feelings is turned upside down. As members of the audience, we do not watch a performance in a detached manner. Our minds, imaginations, and feelings are affected. The mood in which the different strands of the story come together at the end is the mood in which we will go home. It is what we will remember.

A basic question for any director is whether the ending of the play creates harmony. Can the audience go home enjoying a sense of peace and security?

The special occasion of a royal wedding brings together the Duke and some of his least important subjects, a group of workmen. This seems, at first, a satisfying event, but the response that PETER QUINCE and his actors earn for their performance is disappointing. The lovers laugh at their efforts, so the gulf between the **Court** and working men is not properly bridged. Actors have a choice about how they say the lines. For example, Hippolyta's line, "This is the silliest stuff that ever I heard," can be said in a sneering or an affectionate way.

The contemporary director Peter Hall chose to express a final sense of harmony between the different elements in the play. THESEUS sincerely thanked the players and acknowledged the good-hearted loyalty behind the performance of *Pyramus and Thisbe*. Everyone enjoyed the **Bergamask** dance. The blessing of the house and the new marriages by the FAIRIES represented an inner harmony, bringing peace, rest, and good fortune.

For actors or members of the audience, *A Midsummer Night's Dream* offers choices about how much the deep motives of our lives are uncovered. It offers choices about how hopeful and positive we can be. Exploring those choices is an adult activity. *A Midsummer Night's Dream* is definitely not just for children.

GLOSSARY

bellows mender someone who repairs a bellows, which is a device used for blowing fires or sounding an organ

bergamask also spelled bergamasque; a country dance, originally associated with the town of Bergamo, Italy

bower shelter of leafy branches

Court family, household, or followers of a king, queen, or member of the royal family

dress circle section of theater seats originally reserved for people who were in formal clothing

Elizabethan relating to Queen Elizabeth I of England and her reign, from 1533–1603

epilogue speech or poem at the end of a play in which one of the characters speaks to the audience

farce play that is full of silliness and unreal situations, meant to be very funny

gallery highest balcony in a theater

joiner carpenter who makes doors, windows, and other inside woodwork

masque entertainment with fine costumes and scenery performed in England in the 1500s and 1600s

nunnery community of nuns and the building in which they live

page youth who is a servant to a person of high rank

parody funny imitation of serious writing

text original words of a writer

tinker person who repairs pots and pans, usually wandering from place to place to do business

Victorian relating to England's Queen Victoria and her reign, from 1837 to 1901

MORE BOOKS TO READ

Claybourne, Anna and Rebecca Treays. *World of Shakespeare.* Tulsa, Okla.: E.D.C. Publishing, 1997.

Ganeri, Anita. *Young Person's Guide to Shakespeare.* San Diego, Calif.: Harcourt, 1999.

Morley, Jacqueline. *Shakespeare's Theater.* Lincolnwood, Ill.: NTC Contemporary Publishing Company, 1994.

Olster, Fredi (ed.). *A Midsummer Night's Dream: A Workbook for Students.* Lyme, N.H.: Smith & Kraus, Incorporated, 1996

Pollinger, Gina (ed.).*Something Rich & Strange: A Treasury of Shakespeare's Verse.* New York: Larousse Kingfisher Chambers, Incorporated, 1995.

Shakespeare, William. *A Midsummer Night's Dream.* New York: Simon & Schuster Trade, 1999.

Stanley, Diane. *The Bard of Avon.* New York: Morrow, William & Company, Incorporated, 1998.

ADDITIONAL RESOURCES

African-American Shakespeare Company
5214-F Diamond Heights Blvd.
PMB 923
San Francisco, CA 94131
Tel: (415) 333-1918
This company's mission is to produce European classical works with an African-American cultural perspective

The Shakespeare Theatre
516 8th Street SE
Washington, DC 20003
(202) 547-3230

One of the top Shakespeare companies in the U.S., its mission is to produce and preserve classical theater and to develop new audiences for classical theater.

INDEX